Under the Ice: A New Frontier

Uncovering the conspiracy theory about a German colony deep in Antarctica exploring the universe

Written by Peyton Cottrell II

Peyton Cottrell II
1919 Potomac St.
Houston, Texas 77057

First Paperback Edition: December 2018

Cottrell II, Peyton, 1970-
Under the Ice: A New Frontier : by Peyton Cottrell II - 1st ed.

Summary: "Under the Ice: A New Frontier" explores the conspiracy theory that Germany has settled a colony two miles underground and secretly building flying saucers to explore worlds beyond the Milky Way.

ISBN: 9781790768684

{1. Conspiracy Theory. 2. Antarctica. 3. Germany. 4. Space Travel.}

Printed in the United States of America

This book was inspired by and dedicated to:

Holly Albertson, Melissa Erekson, Gracie Esparza, Flavis Pierce and Sandra Pierce

Table of Contents

The Research

Europeans are thinking about leaving Europe and

rebuilding their ancestors' homeland in Antarctica. I'm a

very strong psychic and the spirits have told me that

there will be several thousands of Europeans that have

gotten too irritated at the European Union politics and

they will be relocating to the frozen continent within a decade to a few years.

I was looking on YouTube several months ago at the unique German cultures (or enclaves), and I was very shocked to see one enclave that's in the South Pole. I did some investigating, and I have recently discovered that Deusctchland (German) knew in 1942 that they were going to lose World War II that ended in 1945 but the German Government were the only politicians that did surrender!

The entire Nazis party fled to South America and mostly to the South Pole, and the allies did make a compromise with the Nazis Party in 1967 that has been renamed as Neu Schwabenland (or New Swabia... comes from a Southern state in the European Continental Germany).

The compromise stated that the Neu Schwabenlanders can control Antarctica at two miles below the ice, they (Neu Swabians) can have a base on the dark side of the moon, and the Neu Swabians can have a secretive seat in the United Nations.

The Nazis that fled to the South Pole did win the last battle of World War II that was fought in 1946 that was called Operation Highjump. That victory gave these radical Germans an opportunity to build a giant city they called Neu Berlin at two miles under the ice. Their main industry in the Second Germany/Neu Schwabenland, South Pole, is to manufacture anti-gravity propulsion systems (flying saucers). They are the first nation in the

1940s that invented man-made flying saucers. They have factories in Antarctica and Brazil, and they have 70 years of experience in mass producing flying saucers. The Americans have been learning from the New Swabians how to manufacture flying saucers.

There are about 200 videos that are on YouTube about the Second Germany, South Pole, that are called, Base 211, New Swabia, Neu Berlin, and Neu Schwabenland. There are different authors and a clothing line that recognize this European nation that's been hiding since 1945 for political reasons until 2015. Second Germany has 2 million people, and they are the only nation that has expanded their boundaries to other planets in the Milky Way Galaxy! Second Germany,

South Pole, does mainly spend most of their time traveling in flying saucers amongst the stars.

I have been asked one time by a Texan, since the people of Second Germany are technologically superior to us, why didn't they fight us again? My reasoning is the New Swabians believe that it's far more meaningful to travel amongst the galaxies, meet the different alien life forms and to expand their German nation on the different galaxies. They want to enjoy their lives in the universe rather than keep attacking their former World War II allied enemies. The Reptilian Alien base that's also hidden at a few miles under Antarctica along with the German psychics did give the Nazis the technology to learn how to build the Earth's first flying saucers.

German flying saucers do travel to the foreign nations far more than the Earth does realize, and they do know a tremendous amount about the infrastructure of the scientific make up of how to build these flying saucers far more than most of the Americans do because the Germans have been building flying saucers for more than 70 years.

I'm a patriotic Texan and an American, and there is a very strong chance that Antarctica could be opened for American democratic commerce in a few years, primarily because of the mineral resources, the New Swabians culture. It's a new frontier, and I have heard that Neu Schwabenland is slowly becoming a democratic county!

This is one of the greatest archaeological

discoveries of the 21st Century!

World War II officially ended in 1967 with a

compromise for Neu Schwabenland!

References

YouTube Videos:

UFOs and Extraterrestrials - German UFO Base in Brazil
https://youtu.be/OnkExyH2jc8

New Swabian Bases: The Secret Antarctic Colony –

Robert Sepehr

https://youtu.be/o625nlqj8LQ

Secret Space Program Disclosure – Robert Sepehr

https://www.youtube.com/watch?v=NKnqx1IfpN4&feature=youtu.be

Antarctica Nazi underground base found on

Google Earth in New Swabia

https://www.youtube.com/watch?v=mtZ6yGPvHuc&feature=youtu.be

Book:

"Empire Beneath the Ice:

How the Nazis Won World War II"

by Steve Quayle

http://www.stevequayle.com/index.php?s=624

See Peyton Cottrell's other books:

The Bone Orchard

The Symbols of Jefferson Davis Hospital

Under the Ice

Antarctica: What's Next

The Secrets of Goliad, Texas

Viking Highway in Harris County, Texas

Buried Catholic Church in New Orleans
and Forbidden Holy Statues

All available on

Amazon

About the Author

Peyton Cottrell II started ghosthunting in 2002 because he felt he could get closer to God if he started talking to people that were having paranormal experiences every day. His strategy worked. He was impressed by the large number of paranormal investigation groups in his hometown of Houston, Texas. Through these groups, Cottrell learned and reviewed the scientific evidence of the Third Eye, leading him to study the ways spirits communicate from beyond the grave.

His interest in the historic building in downtown Houston formerly known as Jefferson Davis Hospital inspired filmmaker Billy S. Cox to write a script, which was later re-imagined into a fictional book by Elaine Sallerrot called "The Bone Orchard."

Cottrell has been continuously haunted by spirits whose bodies lie buried beneath the historic hospital. In "The Symbols of Jefferson Davis Hospital," he describes his findings after interviewing psychics and white witches, figuring out all the different ways - including symbols and other psychic mediums - these spirits try to communicate from beyond their forgotten graves.

In his 2018 effort, "Under the Ice: A New Frontier," Cottrell briefly explores the conspiracy theory that Germany has an underground colony in Antarctica and is secretly exploring the universe.

In 2019, Cottrell published his follow-up to "Under the Ice" called "Antarctica: What's Next?" as well as "The Secrets of Goliad, Texas," "Viking Highway in Harris County, Texas," and "Buried Catholic Church in New Orleans and Forbidden Holy Statues."

For more information and upcoming books, visit www.amazon.com/author/peytoncottrell.

Made in the USA
Middletown, DE
14 September 2022